POP HITS
FOR ACCORDION

ARRANGED BY GARY MEISNER

ISBN 978-1-5400-1447-4

Visit Hal Leonard Online at
www.halleonard.com

Contact Us:
Hal Leonard
7777 West Bluemound Road
Milwaukee, WI 53213
Email: info@halleonard.com

In Europe contact:
Hal Leonard Europe Limited
42 Wigmore Street
Marylebone, London, W1U 2RN
Email: info@halleonardeurope.com

In Australia contact:
Hal Leonard Australia Pty. Ltd.
4 Lentara Court
Cheltenham, Victoria, 3192 Australia
Email: info@halleonard.com.au

ALL OF ME

Words and Music by JOHN STEPHENS
and TOBY GAD

when I lose, I'm win - ning. 'Cause I give you all ___

___ of me, ___ and you give me all ___

___ of you, ___ oh. ___ oh. ___

Give me all ___ of you. ___ Cards on the ta - ble, ___ we're ___

both show - ing — hearts. — Risk - ing it all, though — it's —

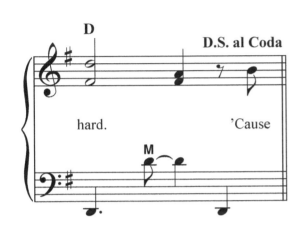

hard. 'Cause

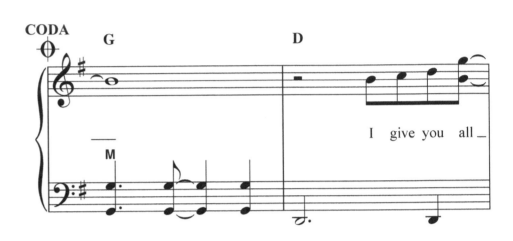

I give you all —

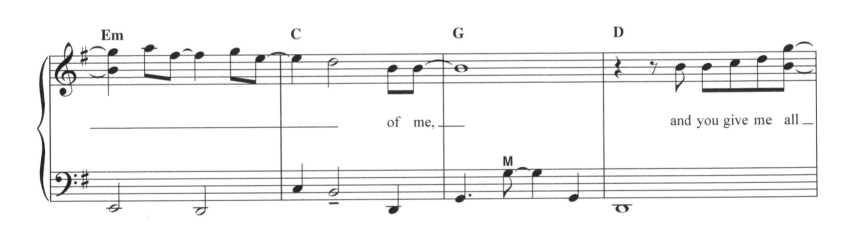

of me, — and you give me all —

of you, — oh. —

CITY OF STARS
from LA LA LAND

Music by JUSTIN HURWITZ
Lyrics by BENJ PASEK & JUSTIN PAUL

Gm ... **C** ... **F** **Am/E**

knows? _____ I felt it from the first em - brace I shared with

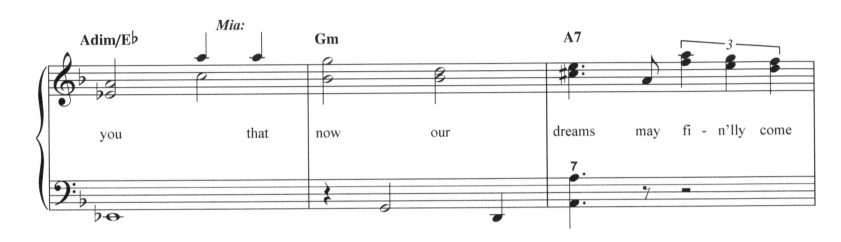

Adim/E♭ *Mia:* **Gm** **A7**

you that now our dreams may fi - n'lly come

Dm **Dm/C** **Gm**

true. _____ Cit - y of stars, _

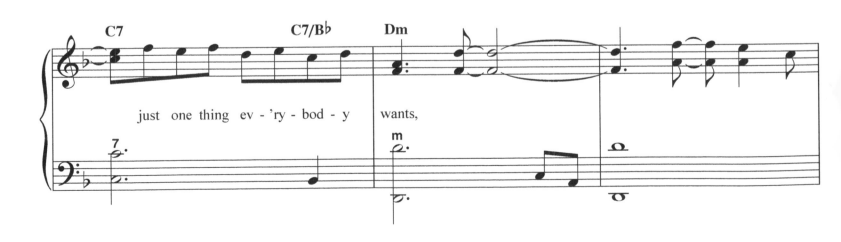

C7 **C7/B♭** **Dm**

just one thing ev - 'ry - bod - y wants,

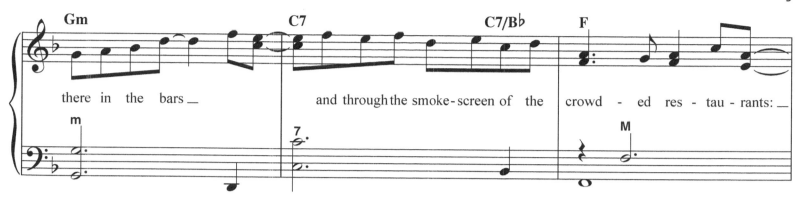

there in the bars __ and through the smoke-screen of the crowd - ed res - tau - rants: __

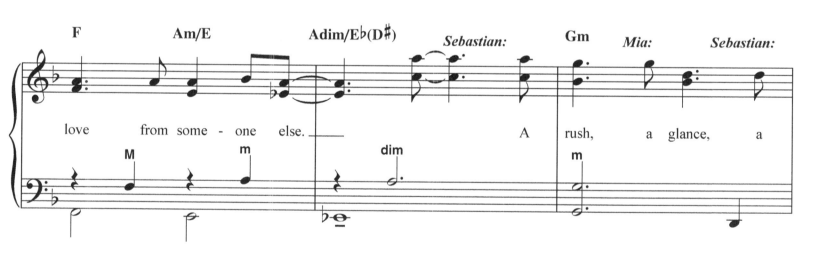

__ it's love. __ Yes, all we're look - ing for is

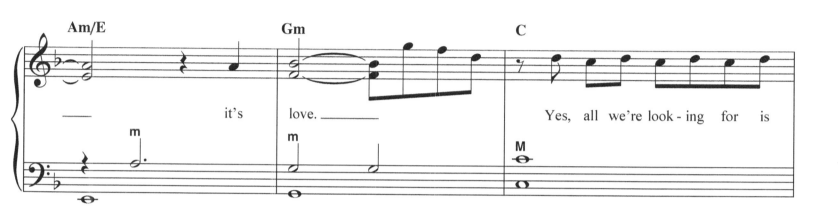

Sebastian: **Mia:** **Sebastian:**

love from some - one else. __ A rush, a glance, a

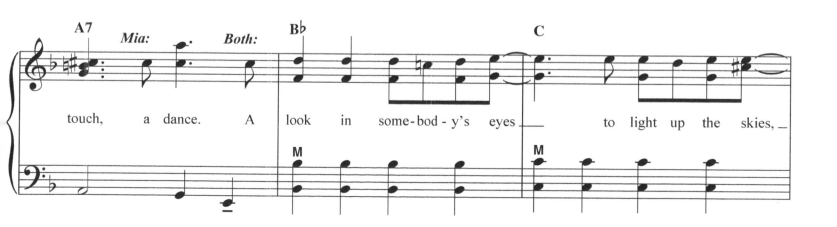

Mia: **Both:**

touch, a dance. A look in some - bod - y's eyes __ to light up the skies, __

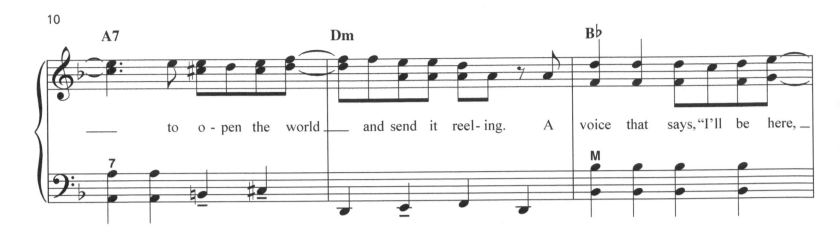

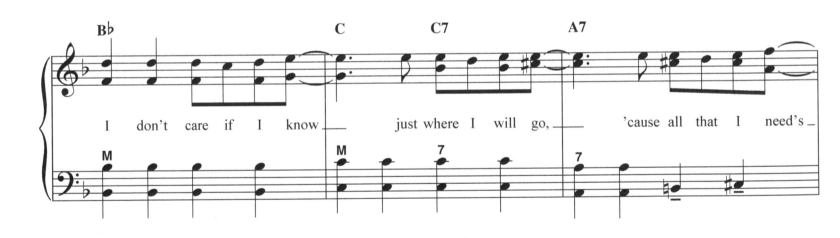

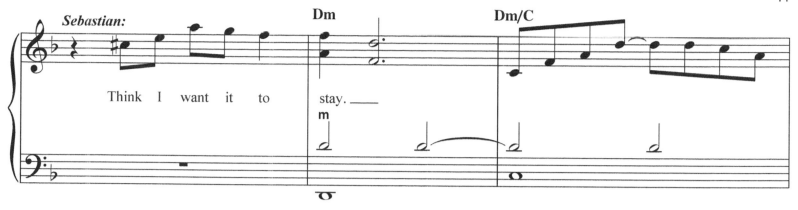

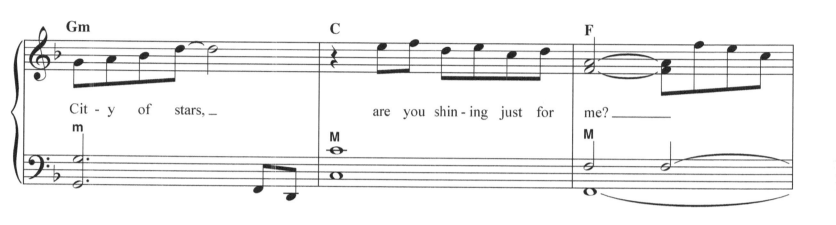

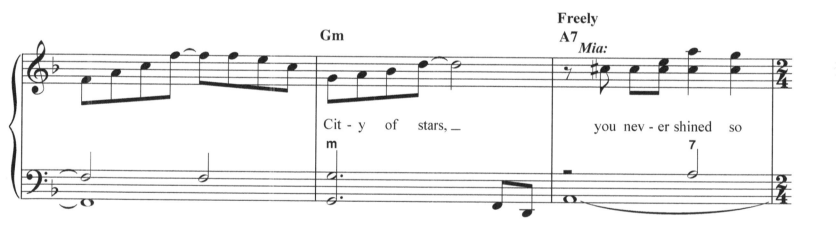

DESPACITO

Words and Music by LUIS FONSI,
ERIKE ENDER, JUSTIN BIEBER,
JASON BOYD, MARTY JAMES GARTON
and RAMÓN AYALA

feel - in' some kind of way.____ Make me wan - na sa - vor ev - 'ry mo - ment

slow - ly, slow - ly._____ You fit me, tai - lor -

made love, how you put it on. ___ Got the on - ly key, know how to turn it on. ___

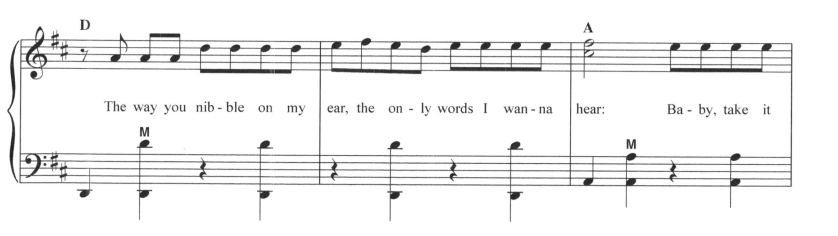

The way you nib - ble on my ear, the on - ly words I wan - na hear: Ba - by, take it

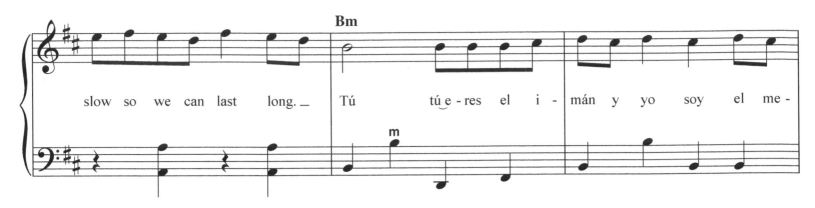

slow so we can last long. __ Tú tú e-res el i - mán y yo soy el me-

tal. Me voy a-cer - can-do y voy ar - man-do el plan. Só - lo con pen-

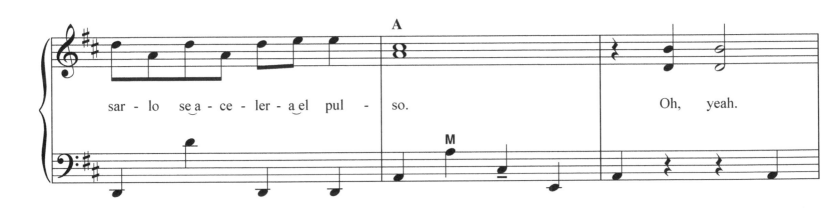

sar - lo se a - ce - ler - a el pul - so. Oh, yeah.

Ya, ya me es - tá gus - tan-do más de lo nor - mal. To - dos mis sen-

ti - dos van pi - dien - do más. Es - to hay que to - mar - lo sin - nin - gún a -

pu - ro. Des - pa - ci - to. Quie - ro res - pi - rar tu cue - llo des - pa - ci -

- to. De - ja que te di - ga so - sas al o - í - do, pa - ra que te a -

cuer - des si no es - tás con - mi - go. Des - pa -

ci - to. Quie-ro des-nu - dar-te a be-sos des - pa - ci - to, fir-mo en las pa-

re-des de tu la - be-rin - to, y ha-cer de tu cuer-po to-do un ma-nu - scri-

- to. _____ Quie-ro ver bai - lar tu pe -

- lo, quie-ro ser tu rit - mo, que le en-se-nes a mi bo -

ci - to. This is how we do it down in Puer - to Ri - co. I just wan - na

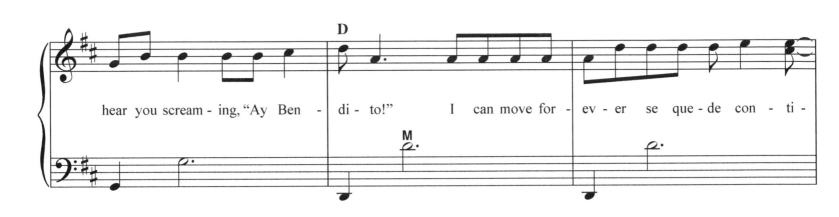

hear you scream - ing, "Ay Ben - di - to!" I can move for - ev - er se que - de con - ti -

- go. _____ Pa - si - to a pa - si - to, sua - ve, sua - ve -

ci - to. Nos va - mos pe - gan - do po - qui - to a po - qui - to

Que le en - se - nes a mi bo -

- ca, tus lu - ga - res fa - vo - ri - tos. _____

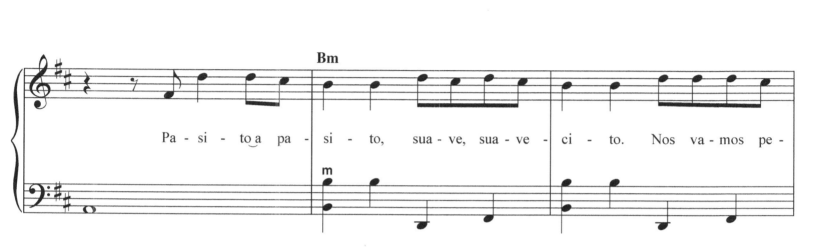

Pa - si - to a pa - si - to, sua - ve, sua - ve - ci - to. Nos va - mos pe -

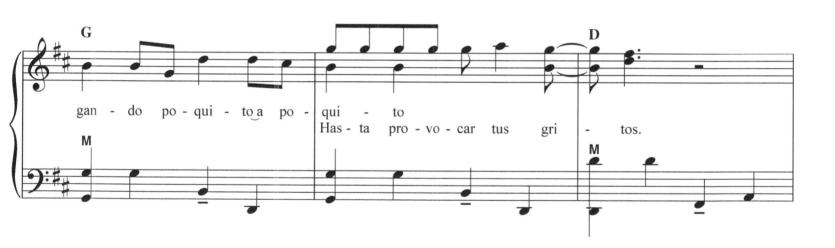

gan - do po - qui - to a po - qui - to
Has - ta pro - vo - car tus gri - tos.

Y que ol - vi - des _ tu a - pe - lli - do. Des - pa - ci - to.

HALLELUJAH

Words and Music by
LEONARD COHEN

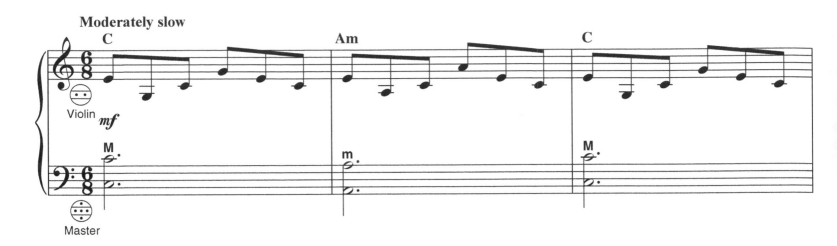

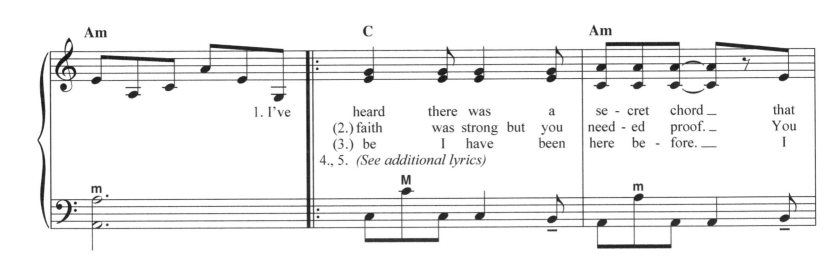

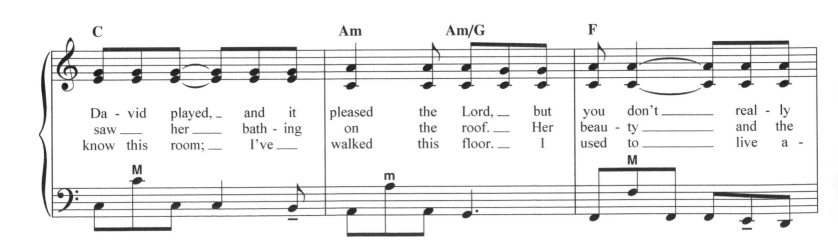

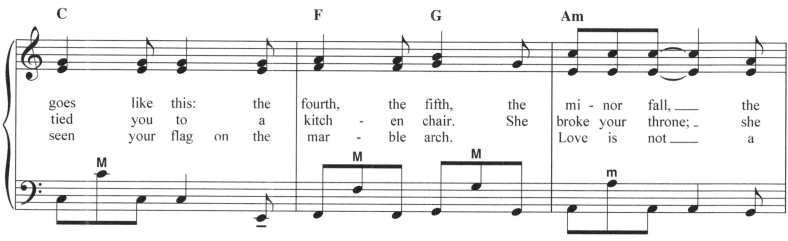

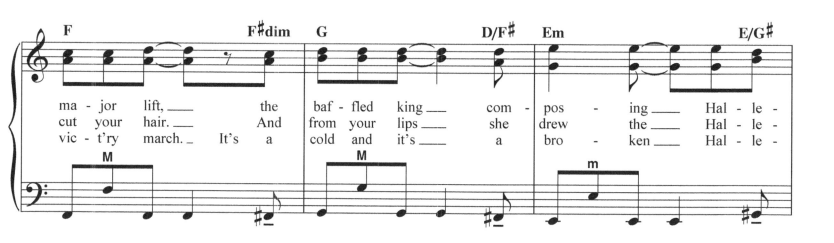

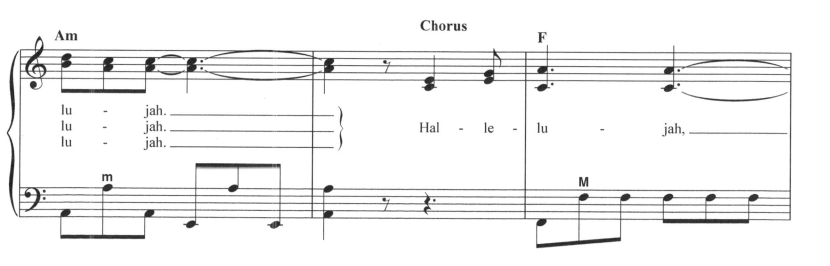

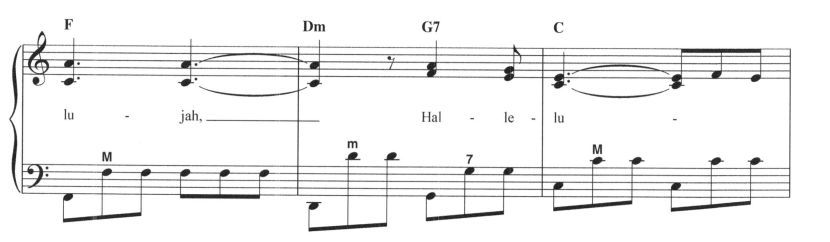

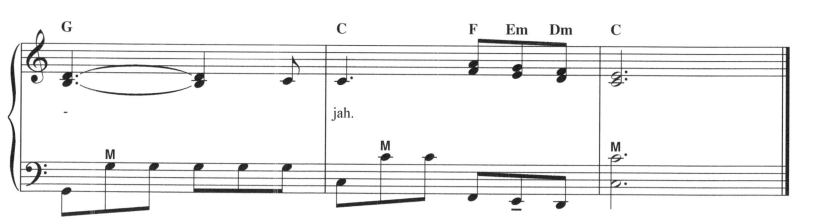

Additional Lyrics

4. There was a time you let me know
   What's real and going on below.
   But now you never show it to me, do you?
   And remember when I moved in you.
   The holy dark was movin', too,
   And every breath we drew was Hallelujah.
   Chorus

5. Maybe there's a God above,
   And all I ever learned from love
   Was how to shoot at someone who outdrew you.
   And it's not a cry you can hear at night.
   It's not somebody who's seen the light.
   It's a cold and it's a broken Hallelujah.
   Chorus

HELLO

Words and Music by ADELE ADKINS
and GREG KURSTIN

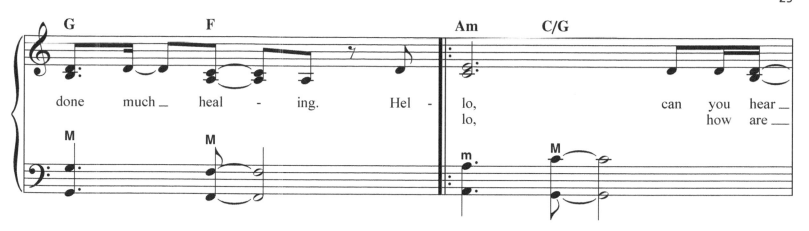

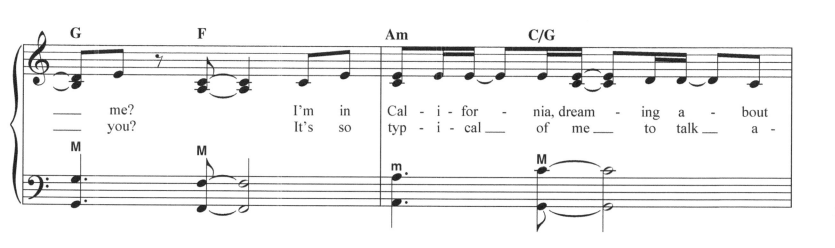

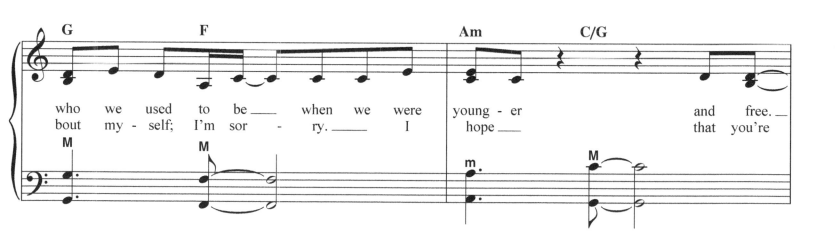

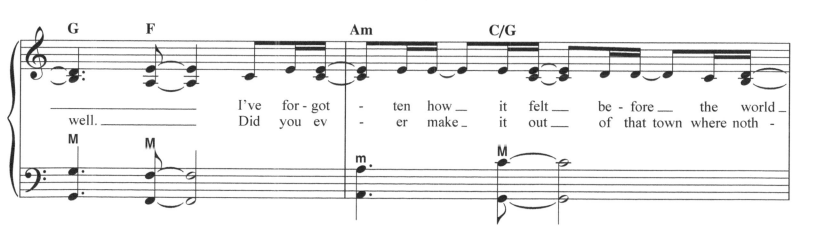

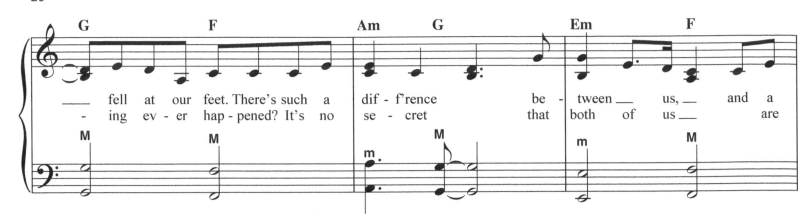

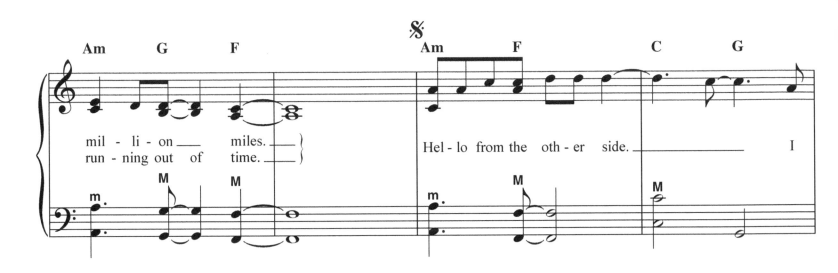

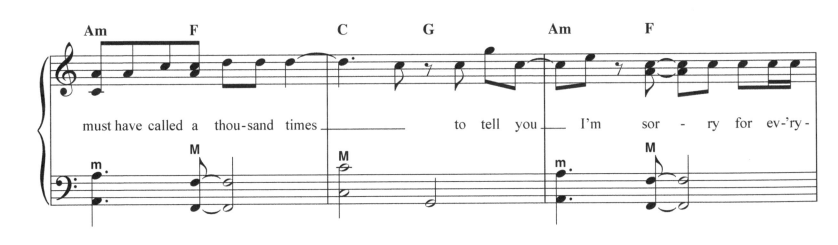

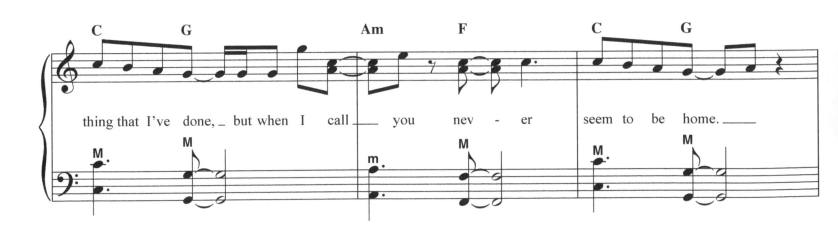

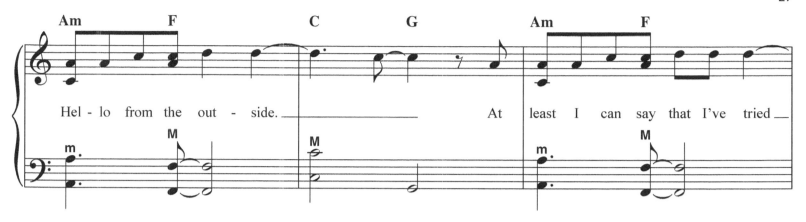

Hel - lo from the out - side. _____ At least I can say that I've tried ___

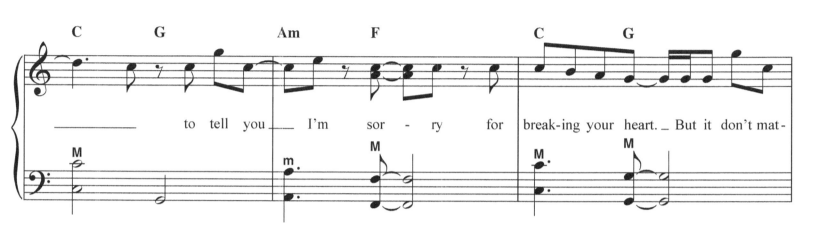

_____ to tell you ___ I'm sor - ry for break - ing your heart. _ But it don't mat-

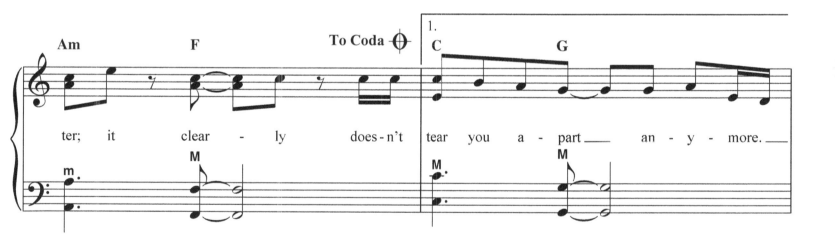

To Coda ⊕ | 1.

ter; it clear - ly does - n't tear you a - part ___ an - y - more. ___

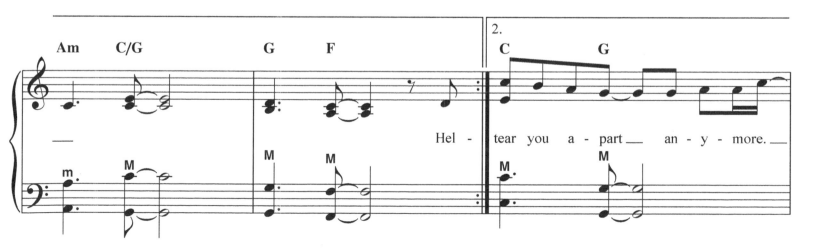

2.

___ Hel - | tear you a - part ___ an - y - more. ___

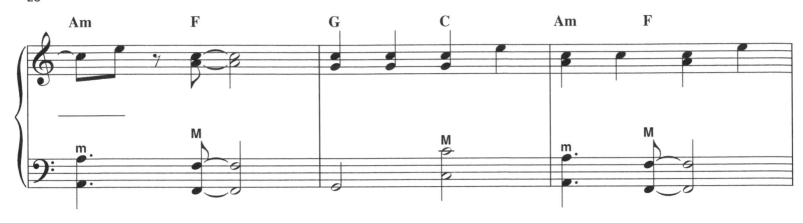

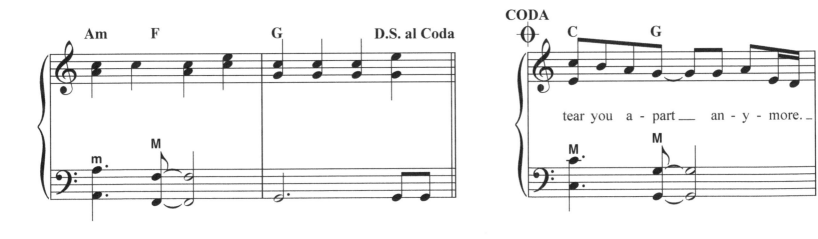

tear you a - part___ an - y - more.___

I'M YOURS

Words and Music by
JASON MRAZ

Well, you done done me in; you bet I felt it. I tried to be chill, but you're so hot that I melt-ed. I

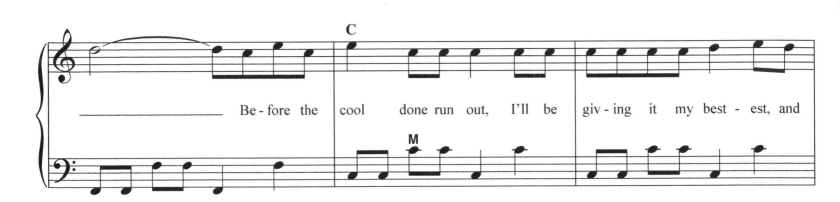

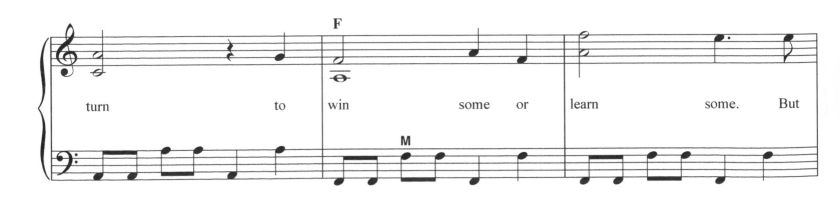

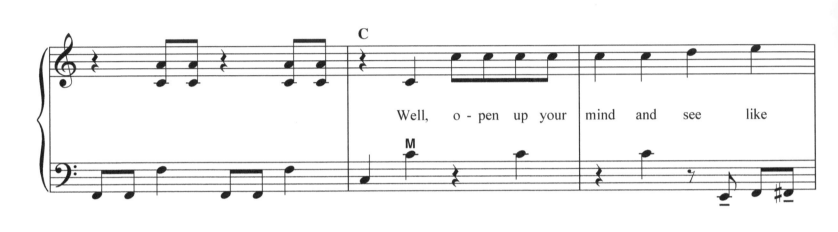

Well, o - pen up your mind and see like

me.   O - pen up your plans and, damn, you're free.   Look in - to your

heart ___ and you'll find   love,   love, _____   love.

Lis - ten to the mu - sic of the mo - ment; peo - ple dance and sing. We're just

one big fam - i - ly, and it's our god - for - sak - en right to be

loved, loved, _____ loved, love, loved. _____

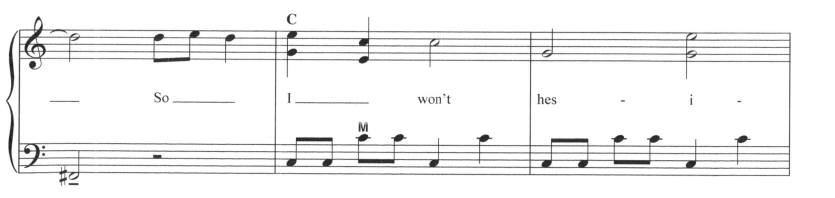

_____ So _____ I _____ won't hes - i -

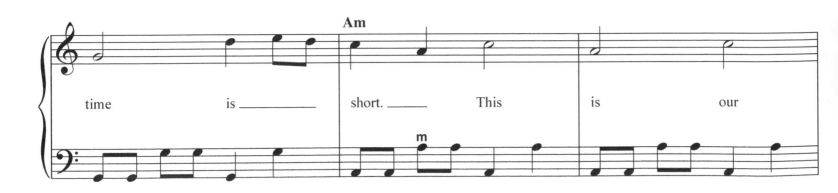

fate. I'm yours. _____

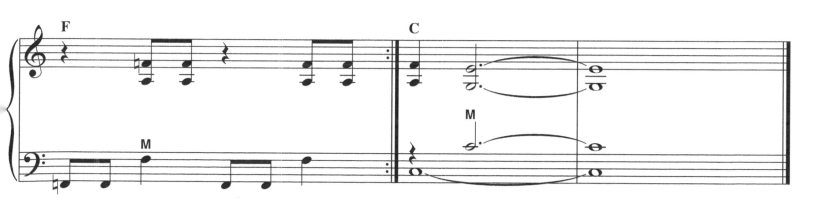

JUST THE WAY YOU ARE

Words and Music by BRUNO MARS,
ARI LEVINE, PHILIP LAWRENCE,
KHARI CAIN and KHALIL WALTON

She's so beau - ti - ful, and I tell her ev - 'ry day.

Yeah, I know, _ I know _ when I com - pli - ment her, she won't be - lieve _ me.

And it's so, ____ it's so ____ sad to think that she don't see what I ____ see.

But ev - 'ry time she asks me, "Do I look o - kay?" I ____ say:

38

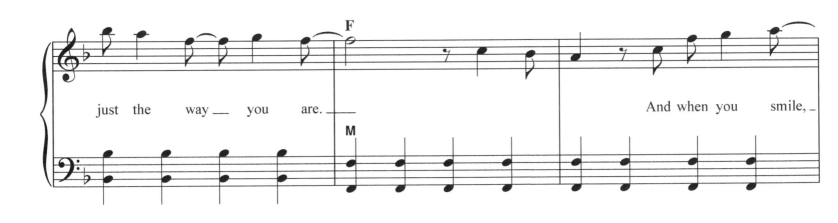

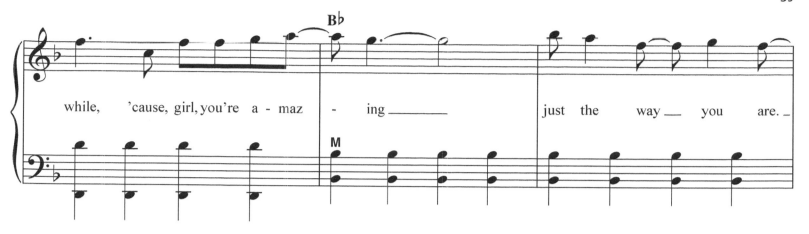

while, 'cause, girl, you're a - maz - ing ____ just the way ___ you are. ___

To Coda ⊕

____ Yeah. ____ Her lips, ___ her lips, ___ I could

kiss them all day if she'd let me. Her laugh, ___ her laugh, ___ she

hates, but I think it's so sex - y. She's so beau - ti - ful, and I tell her ev - 'ry

day.　　　　　　　　　　　　Oh,　you　know, you know, you know I'd nev - er

ask you to change. ＿　If　per-fect's what you're search-in' for, then　just stay the same. ＿　So ＿

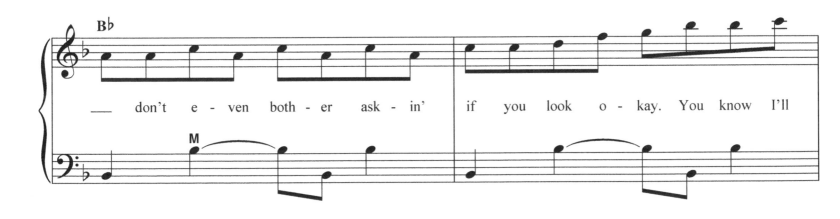

＿　don't e - ven both - er ask - in'　if　you　look　o - kay. You know I'll

say: ＿＿＿＿＿　When I　see your　face, ＿

Yeah. ＿

MY HEART WILL GO ON
(Love Theme From 'Titanic')
from the Paramount and Twentieth Century Fox Motion Picture TITANIC

Music by JAMES HORNER
Lyric by WILL JENNINGS

42

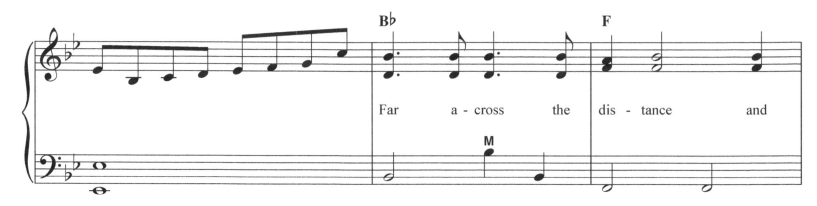

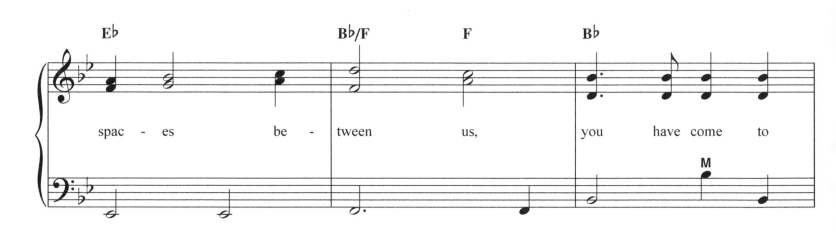

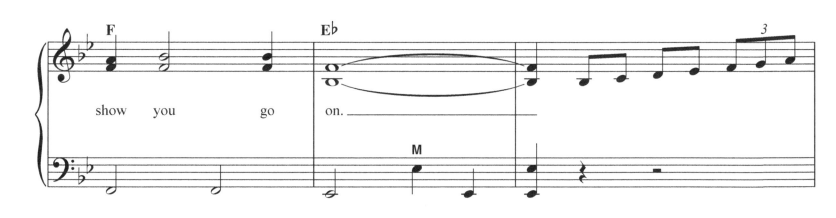

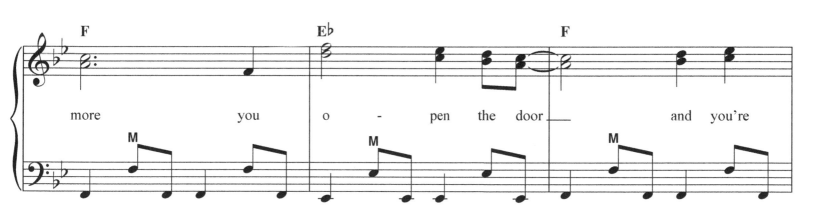

on. *(Instrumental)*

Love can touch us one time and last for a

life - time, and nev - er let go till we're

gone. Love was when I

45

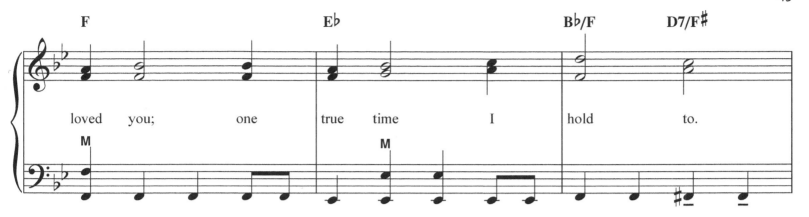

loved you;   one   true   time   I   hold   to.

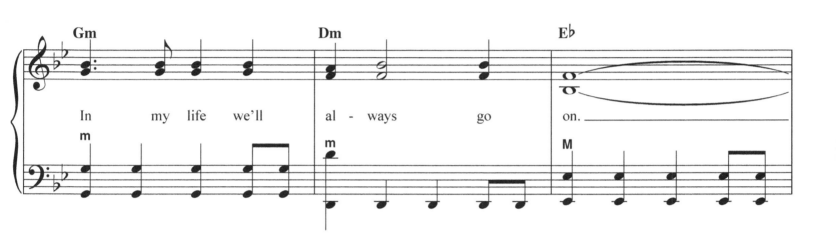

In   my   life   we'll   al - ways   go   on. _____

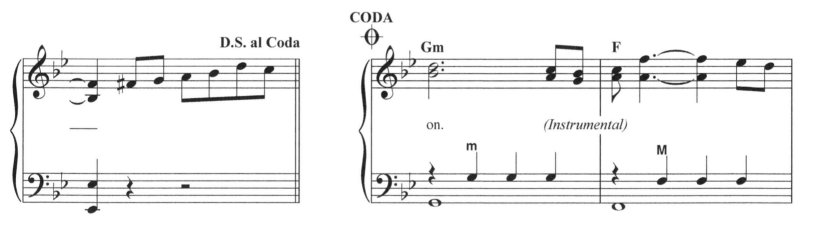

D.S. al Coda

CODA

on.   *(Instrumental)*

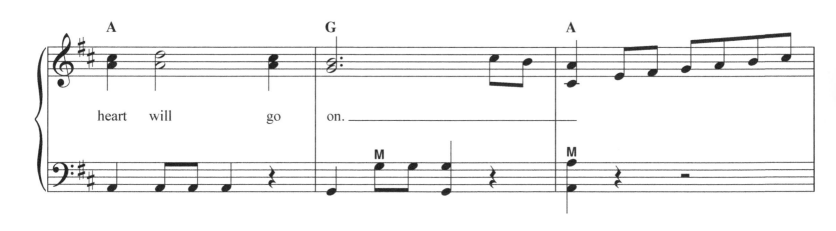

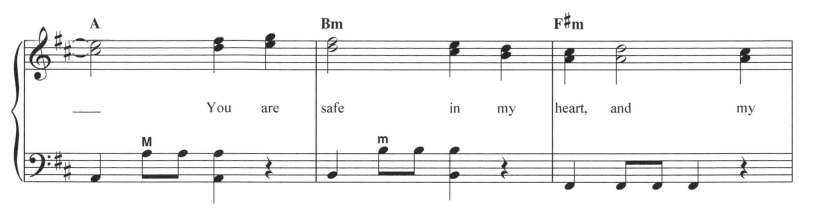

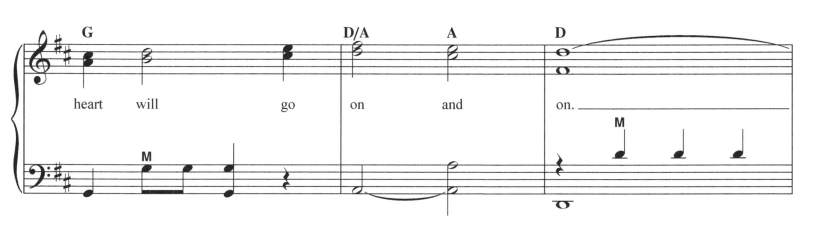

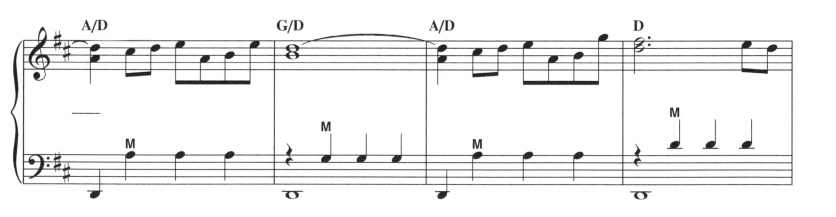

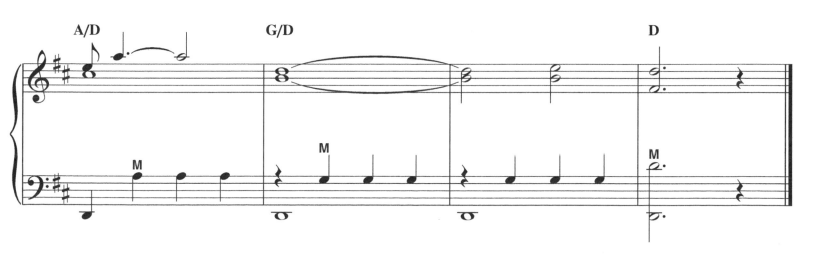

SHAPE OF YOU

Words and Music by ED SHEERAN,
KEVIN BRIGGS, KANDI BURRUSS,
TAMEKA COTTLE, STEVE MAC
and JOHNNY McDAID

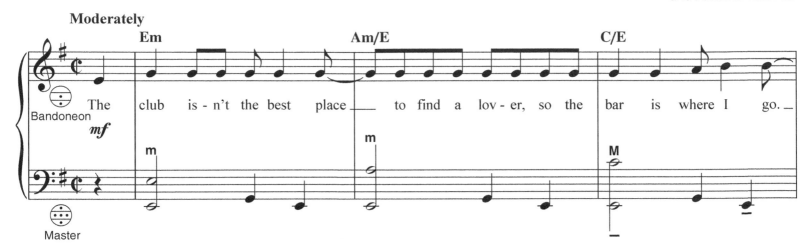

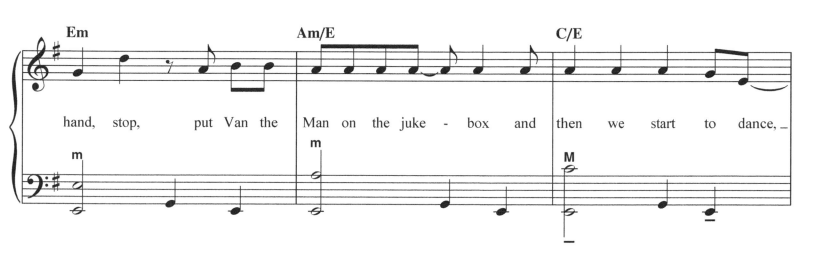

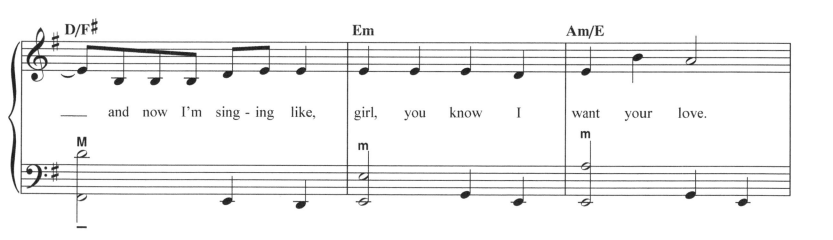

50

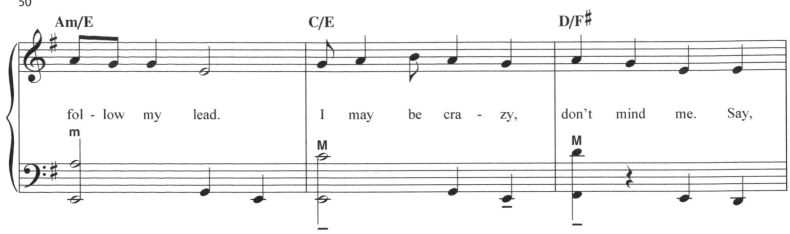

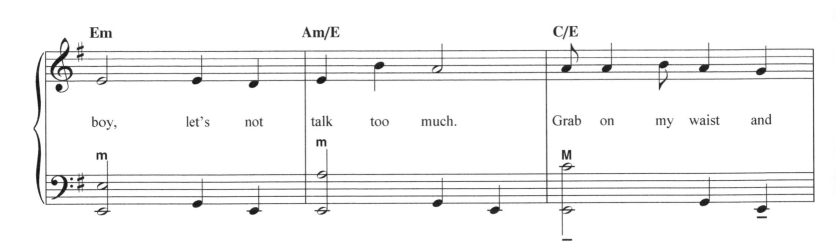

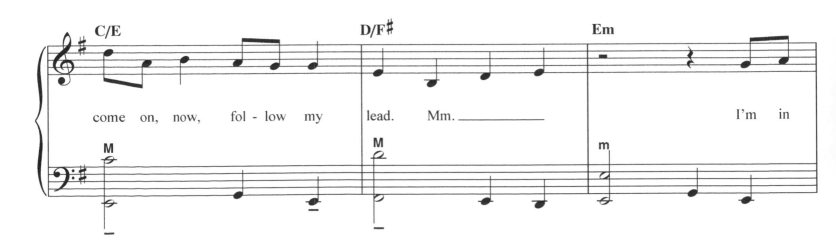

51

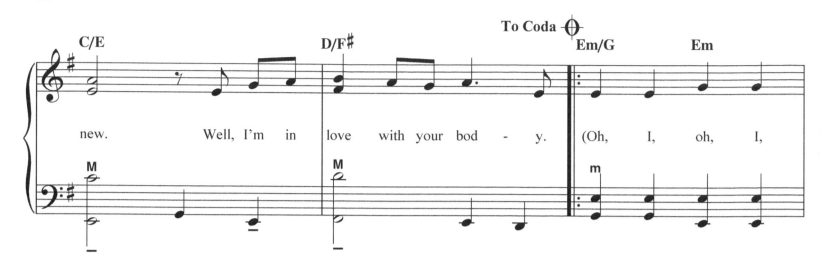

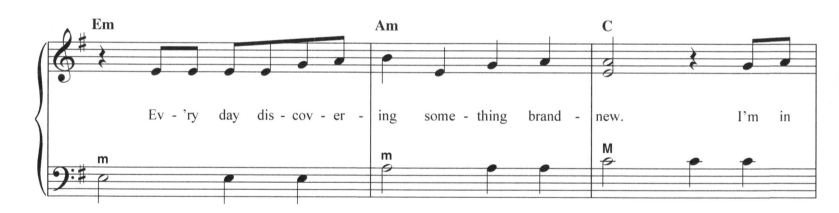

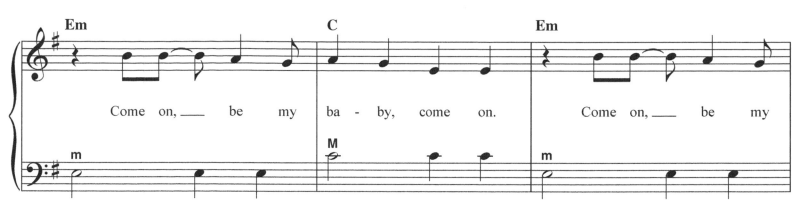

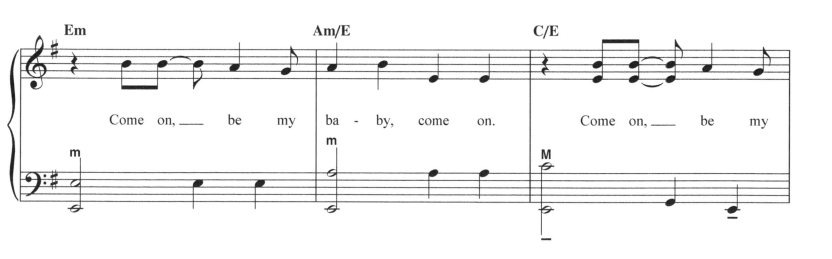

54

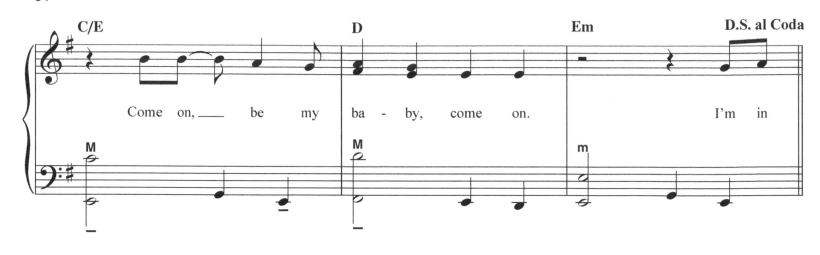

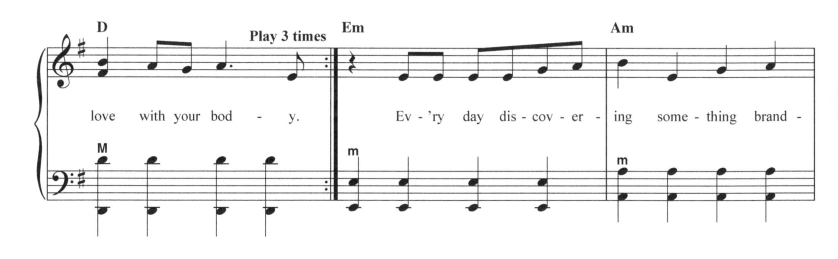

THINKING OUT LOUD

Words and Music by ED SHEERAN
and AMY WADGE

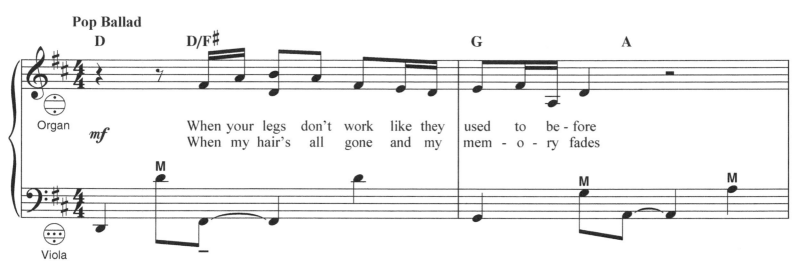

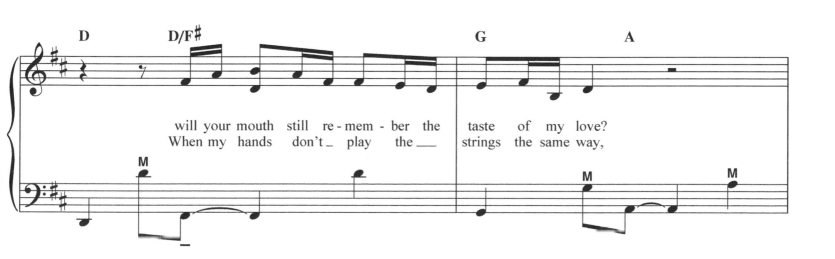

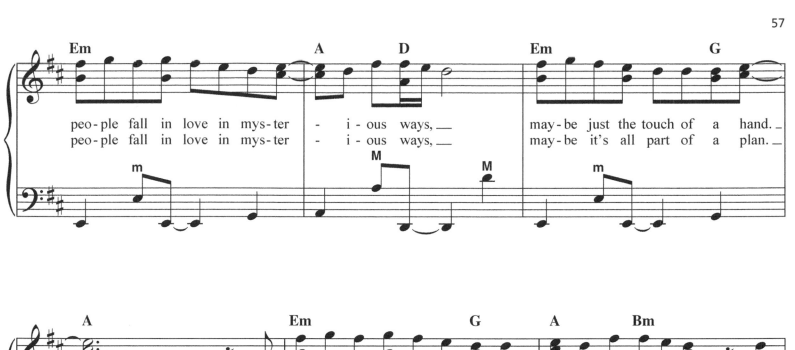

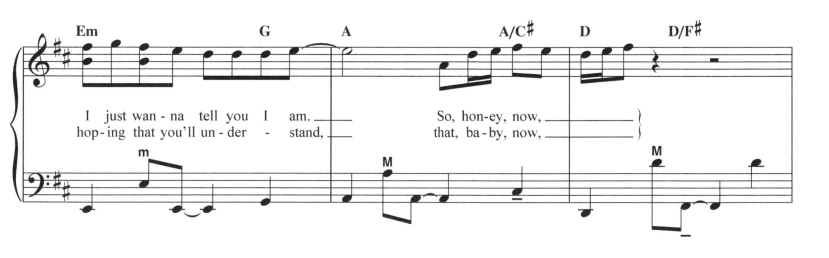

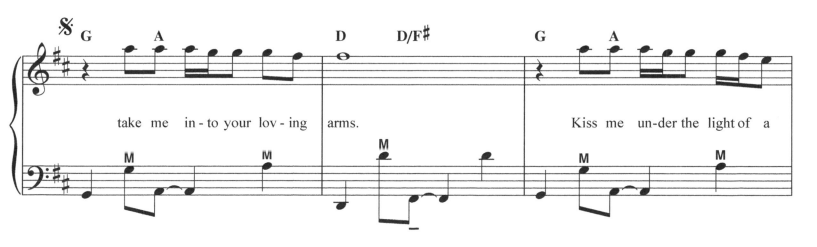

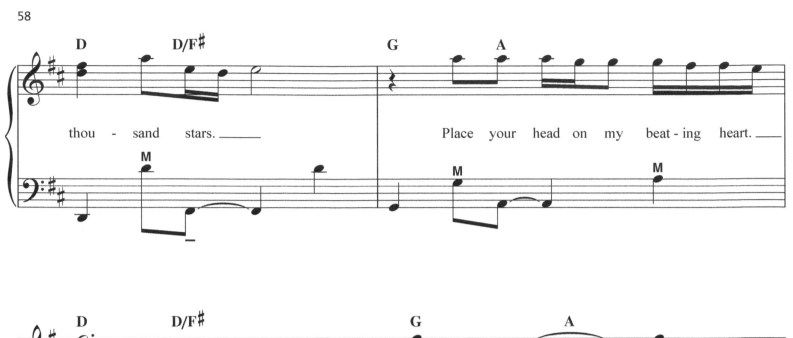

thou - sand stars. _____ Place your head on my beat - ing heart. ____

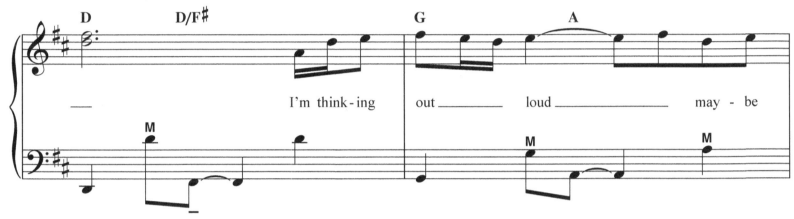

_____ I'm think - ing out _____ loud _____ may - be

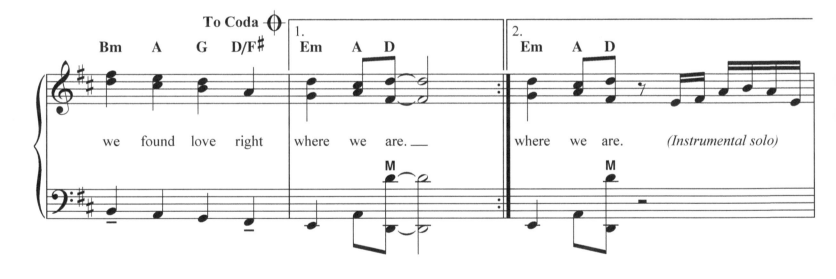

we found love right where we are. ____ where we are. *(Instrumental solo)*

(La, la,

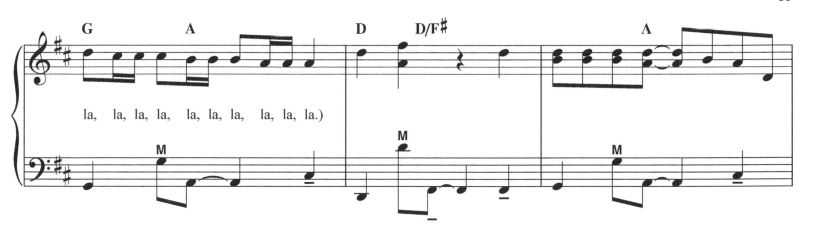

la, la, la, la, la, la, la, la, la, la.)

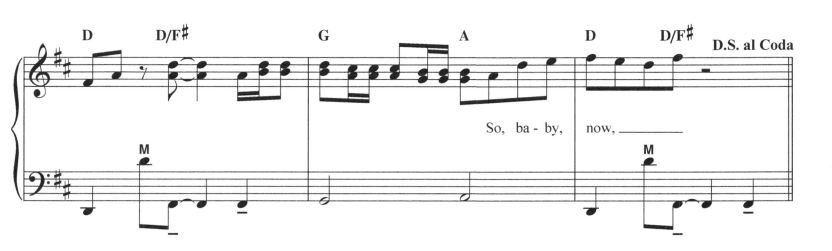

So, ba - by, now, _____

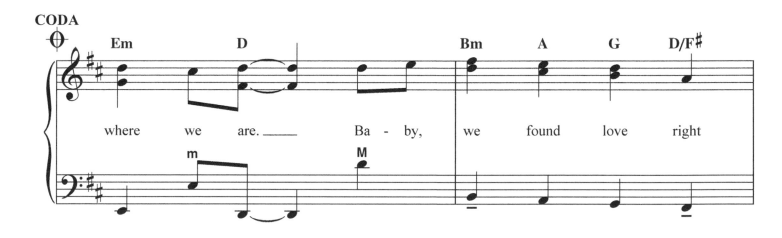

where we are. _____ Ba - by, we found love right

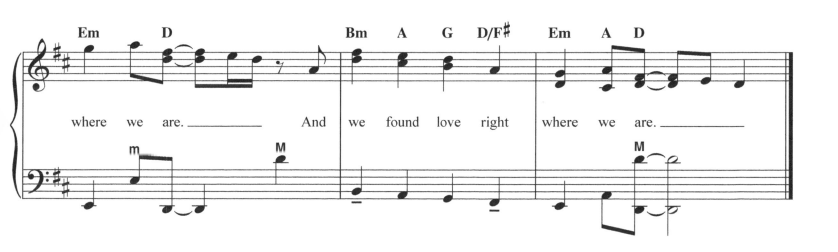

where we are. _____ And we found love right where we are. _____

STAY WITH ME

Words and Music by SAM SMITH,
JAMES NAPIER, WILLIAM EDWARD PHILLIPS,
TOM PETTY and JEFF LYNNE

62

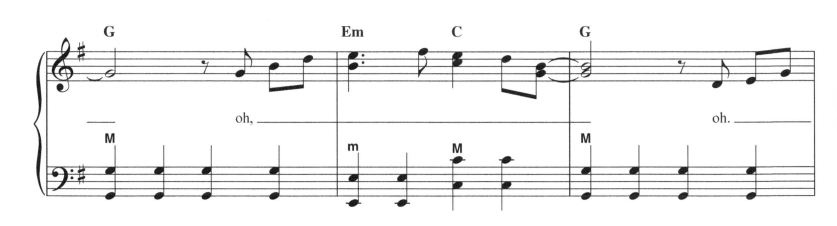

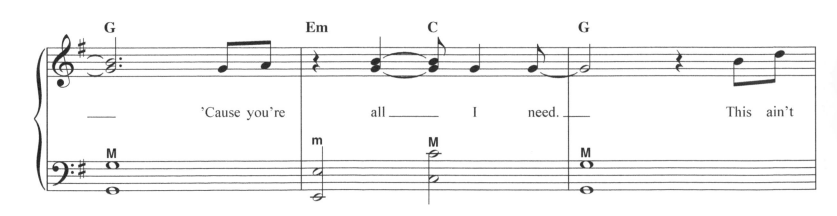

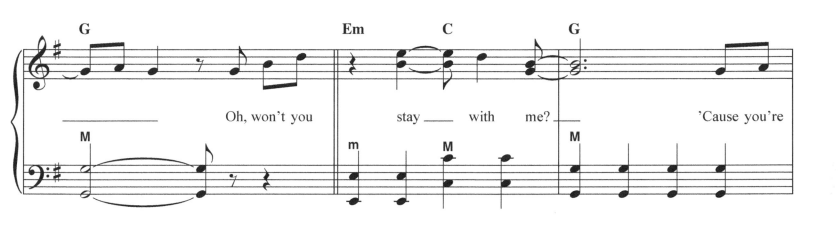

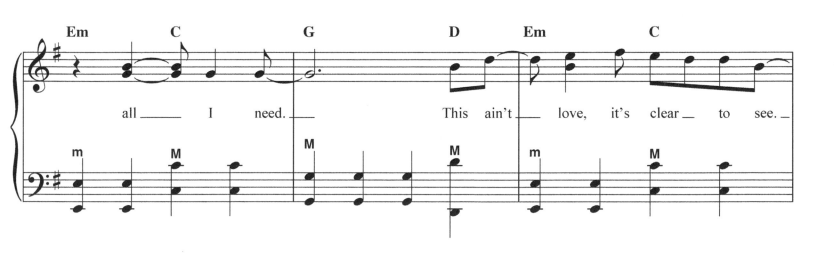

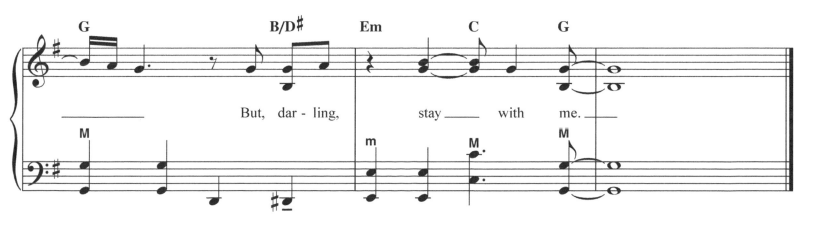

TEARS IN HEAVEN

Words and Music by ERIC CLAPTON
and WILL JENNINGS

65

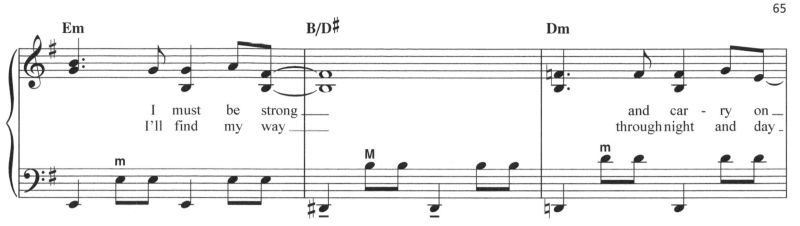

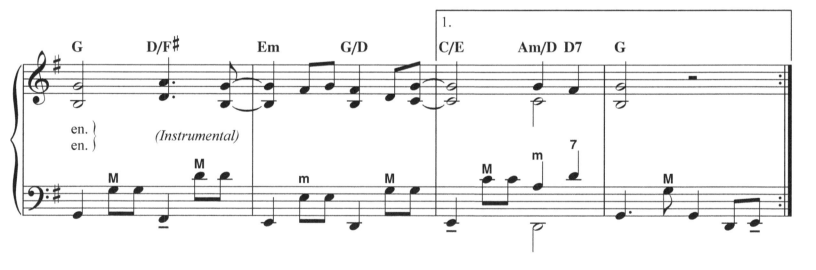

66

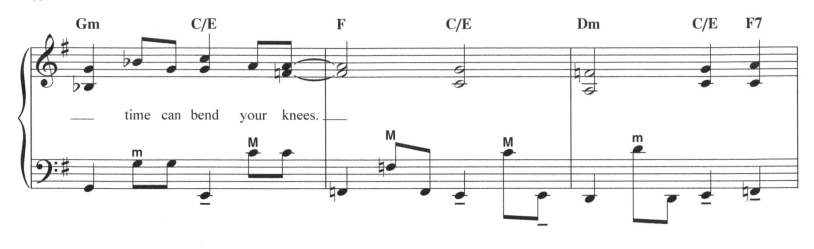

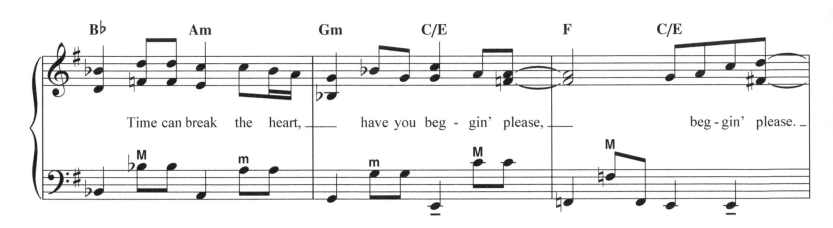

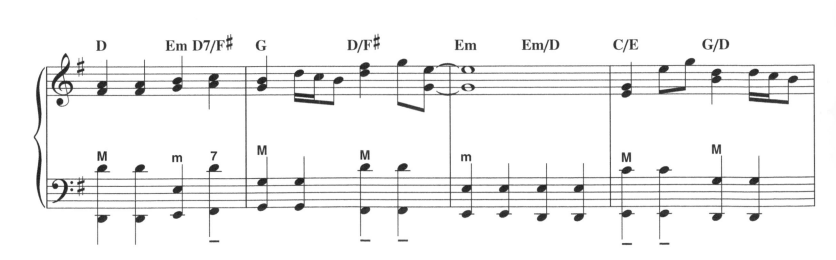

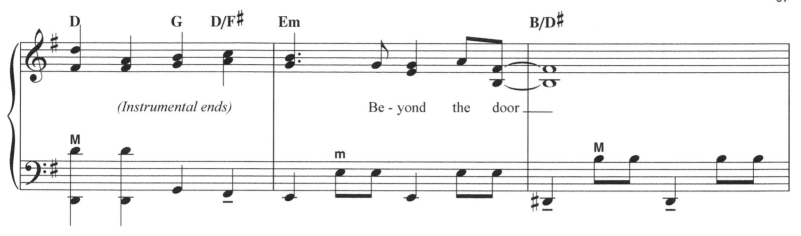

(Instrumental ends) Be - yond the door

there's peace, I'm sure. And I know there'll be no more

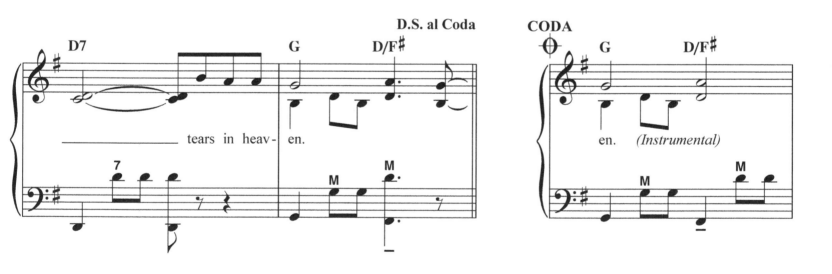

D.S. al Coda

tears in heav- en. CODA en. *(Instrumental)*

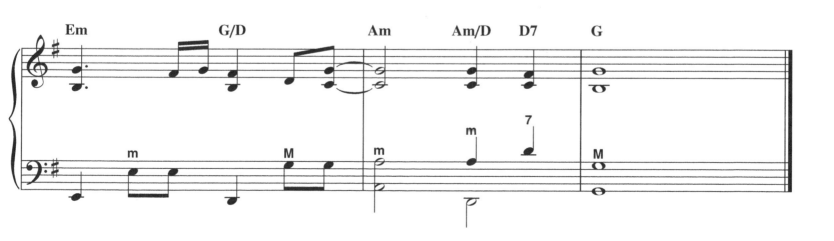

THE WIND BENEATH MY WINGS

from the Original Motion Picture BEACHES

Words and Music by LARRY HENLEY
and JEFF SILBAR

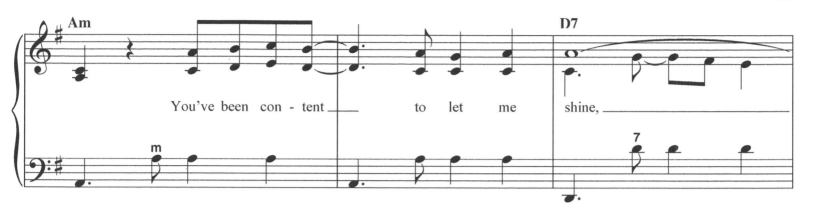

You've been con - tent ____ to let me shine, ____

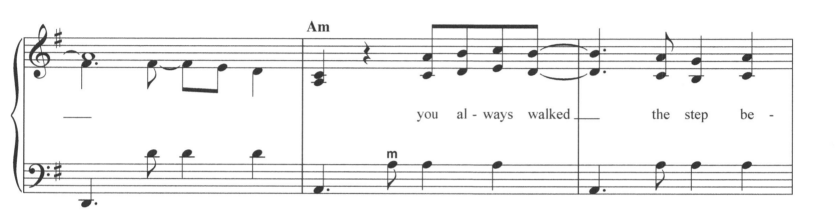

____ you al - ways walked ____ the step be -

hind. ____ I was the one ____

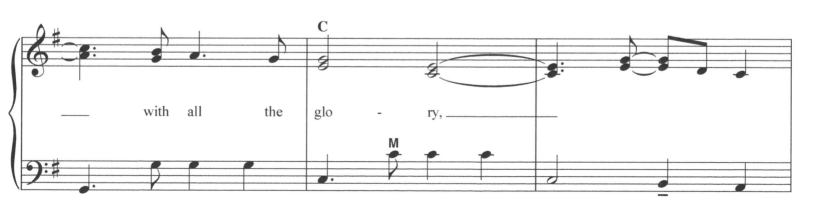

____ with all the glo - ry, ____

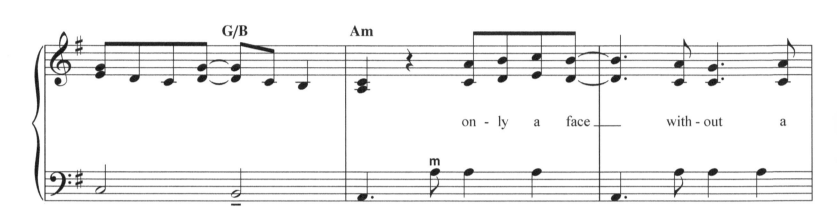

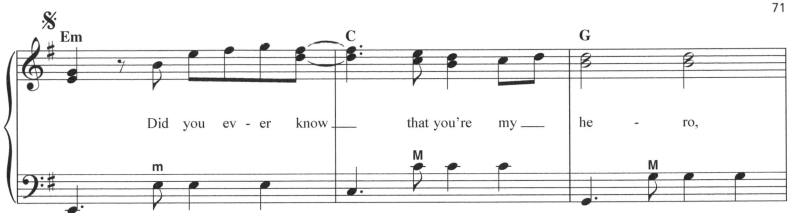

Did you ev - er know ____ that you're my ____ he - ro,

and ev -'ry - thing ____ I'd like to be?

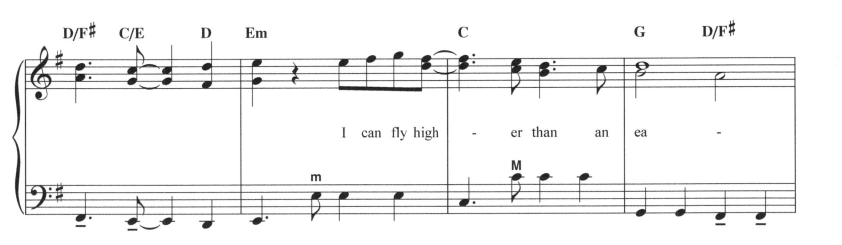

I can fly high - er than an ea -

gle, _____ 'cause you are the wind ____ be - neath my

wings.　*(Instrumental)*

It might have ap - peared _____ to go un - no - ticed _____

_____ that I've got it all _____ here in my heart.

I want you to know _____ I know the

truth:

I would be noth - in' with - out

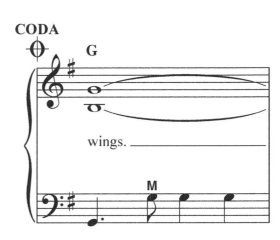

you.   wings.

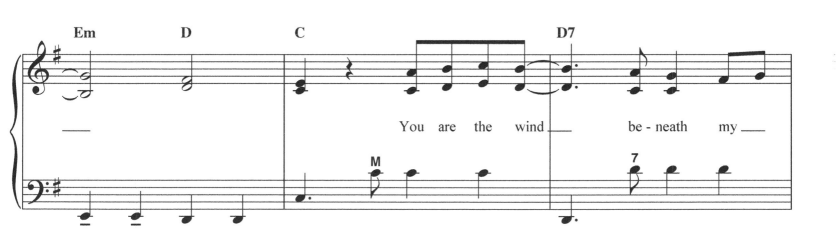

You are the wind   be - neath   my

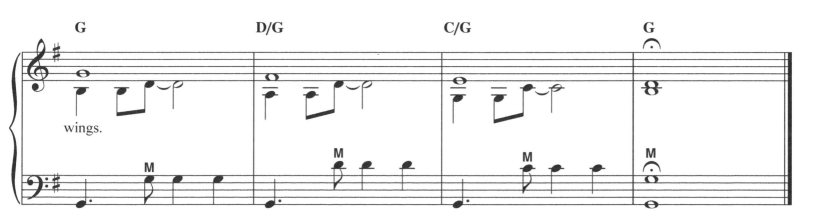

wings.

YOU RAISE ME UP

Words and Music by BRENDAN GRAHAM
and ROLF LOVLAND

still and wait here in the si - lence un - til you come and sit a while with me. _____ You raise me

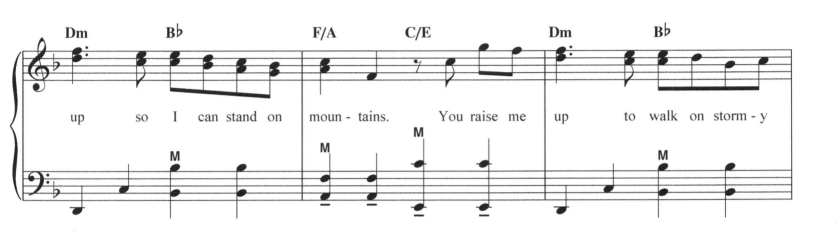

up so I can stand on moun - tains. You raise me up to walk on storm - y

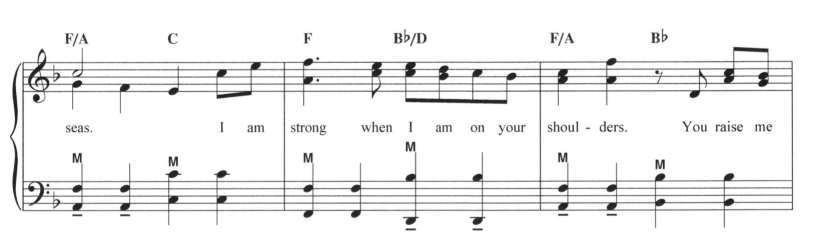

seas. I am strong when I am on your shoul - ders. You raise me

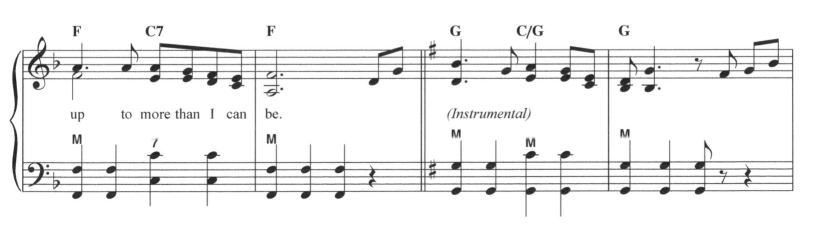

up to more than I can be. *(Instrumental)*

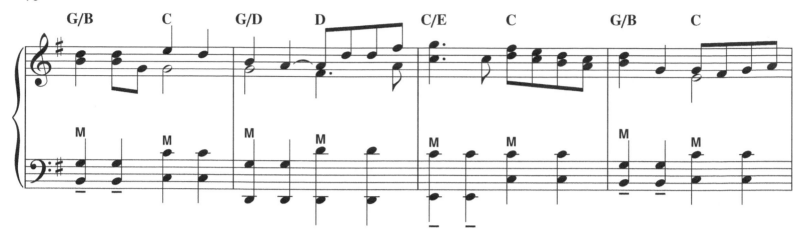

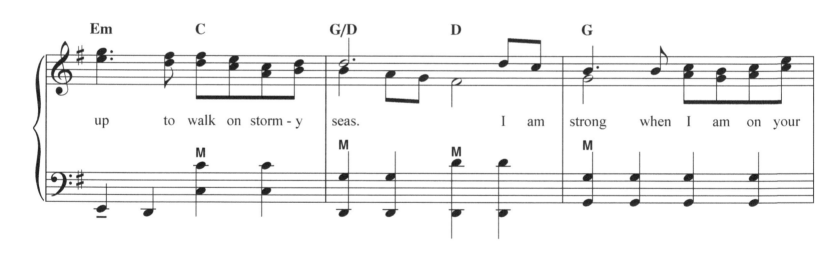

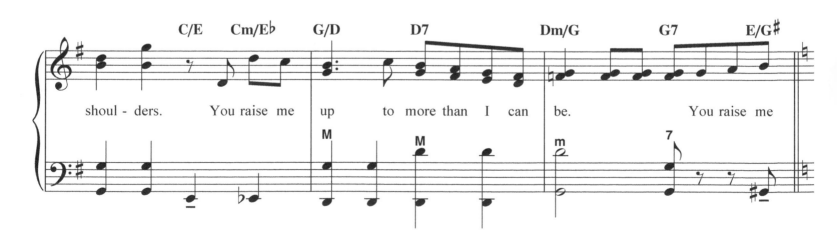

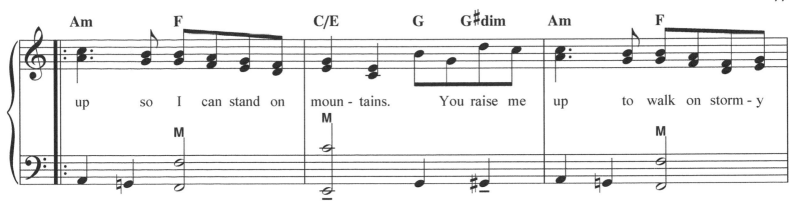

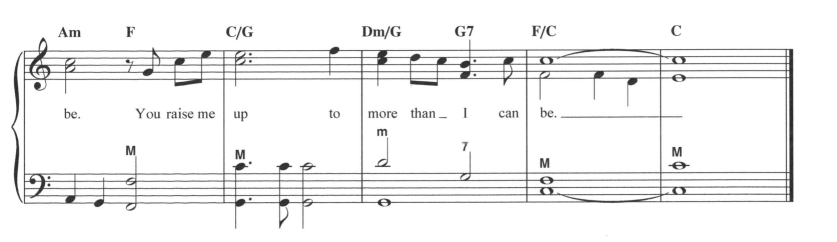

HAL•LEONARD
ACCORDION
PLAY•ALONG

The Accordion Play-Along series features custom accordion arrangements with CD tracks recorded by a live band (accordion, bass and drums). There are two audio tracks for each song – a full performance for listening, plus a separate backing track which lets you be the soloist! The CD is playable on any CD player, and is also enhanced so Mac and PC users can adjust the recording to any tempo without changing the pitch!

1. POLKA FAVORITES
arr. Gary Meisner
Beer Barrel Polka (Roll Out the Barrel) • Hoop-Dee-Doo • Hop-scotch Polka • Just Another Polka • Just Because • Pennsylvania Polka • Tic-Tock Polka • Too Fat Polka (She's Too Fat for Me).
00701705 Book/CD Pack...$14.99

2. ALL-TIME HITS
arr. Gary Meisner
Edelweiss • Fly Me to the Moon (In Other Words) • I Left My Heart in San Francisco • It's a Small World • Moon River • More (Ti Guarderò Nel Cuore) • Poinciana (Song of the Tree) • When I'm Sixty-Four.
00701706 Book/CD Pack...$14.99

3. CLASSIC SONGS
arr. Gary Meisner
Carnival of Venice • Ciribiribin • Come Back to Sorrento • Fascination (Valse Tzigane) • Funiculi, Funicula • I Love You Truly • In the Good Old Summertime • Melody of Love • Peg O' My Heart • When Irish Eyes Are Smiling.
00701707 Book/CD Pack...$14.99

4. CHRISTMAS SONGS
arr. Gary Meisner
Frosty the Snow Man • Have Yourself a Merry Little Christmas • Here Comes Santa Claus (Right down Santa Claus Lane) • The Most Wonderful Time of the Year • Rudolph the Red-Nosed Reindeer • Santa Claus Is Comin' to Town • Silver Bells • Winter Wonderland.
00101770 Book/CD Pack...$14.99

5. ITALIAN SONGS
arr. Gary Meisner
La Sorella • La Spagnola • Mattinata • 'O Sole Mio • Oh Marie • Santa Lucia • Tarantella • Vieni Sul Mar.
00101771 Book/CD Pack...$14.99

Visit Hal Leonard online at **www.halleonard.com**

A COLLECTION OF ALL-TIME FAVORITES
FOR ACCORDION

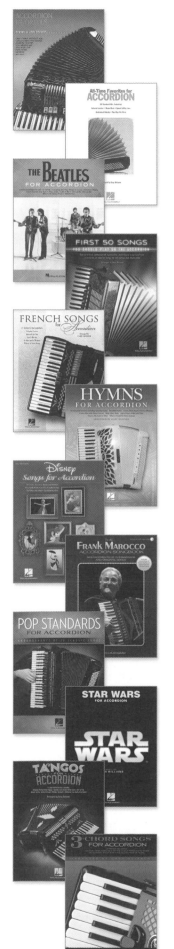

ACCORDION FAVORITES
arr. Gary Meisner

16 all-time favorites, arranged for accordion, including: Can't Smile Without You • Could I Have This Dance • Endless Love • Memory • Sunrise, Sunset • I.O.U. • and more.
00359012...$12.99

ALL-TIME FAVORITES FOR ACCORDION
arr. Gary Meisner

20 must-know standards arranged for accordions. Includes: Ain't Misbehavin' • Autumn Leaves • Crazy • Hello, Dolly! • Hey, Good Lookin' • Moon River • Speak Softly, Love • Unchained Melody • The Way We Were • Zip-A-Dee-Doo-Dah • and more.
00311088...$12.99

THE BEATLES FOR ACCORDION

17 hits from the Lads from Liverpool have been arranged for accordion. Includes: All You Need Is Love • Eleanor Rigby • The Fool on the Hill • Here Comes the Sun • Hey Jude • In My Life • Let It Be • Ob-La-Di, Ob-La-Da • Penny Lane • When I'm Sixty-Four • Yesterday • and more.
00268724 ....$14.99

BROADWAY FAVORITES
arr. Ken Kotwitz

A collection of 17 wonderful show songs, including: Don't Cry for Me Argentina • Getting to Know You • If I Were a Rich Man • Oklahoma • People Will Say We're in Love • We Kiss in a Shadow.
00490157...$10.99

DISNEY SONGS FOR ACCORDION – 3RD EDITION

13 Disney favorites especially arranged for accordion, including: Be Our Guest • Beauty and the Beast • Can You Feel the Love Tonight • Chim Chim Cher-ee • It's a Small World • Let It Go • Under the Sea • A Whole New World • You'll Be in My Heart • Zip-A-Dee-Doo-Dah • and more!
00152508 ....$12.99

FIRST 50 SONGS YOU SHOULD PLAY ON THE ACCORDION
arr. Gary Meisner

If you're new to the accordion, you are probably eager to learn some songs. This book provides 50 simplified arrangements of must-know popular standards, folk songs and show tunes, including: All of Me • Beer Barrel Polka • Carnival of Venice • Edelweiss • Hava Nagila (Let's Be Happy) • Hernando's Hideaway • Jambalaya (On the Bayou) • Lady of Spain • Moon River • 'O Sole Mio • Sentimental Journey • Somewhere, My Love • That's Amore (That's Love) • Under Paris Skies • and more. Includes lyrics when applicable.
00250269 ....$16.99

FRENCH SONGS FOR ACCORDION
arr. Gary Meisner

A très magnifique collection of 17 French standards arranged for the accordion. Includes: Autumn Leaves • Beyond the Sea • C'est Magnifique • I Love Paris • La Marseillaise • Let It Be Me (Je T'appartiens) • Under Paris Skies • Watch What Happens • and more.
00311498...$10.99

HYMNS FOR ACCORDION
arr. Gary Meisner

24 treasured sacred favorites arranged for accordion, including: Amazing Grace • Beautiful Savior • Come, Thou Fount of Every Blessing • Crown Him with Many Crowns • Holy, Holy, Holy • It Is Well with My Soul • Just a Closer Walk with Thee • A Mighty Fortress Is Our God • Nearer, My God, to Thee • The Old Rugged Cross • Rock of Ages • What a Friend We Have in Jesus • and more.
00277160 ....$9.99

ITALIAN SONGS FOR ACCORDION
arr. Gary Meisner

17 favorite Italian standards arranged for accordion, including: Carnival of Venice • Ciribiribin • Come Back to Sorrento • Funiculi, Funicula • La donna è mobile • La Spagnola • 'O Sole Mio • Santa Lucia • Tarantella • and more.
00311089...$9.95

LATIN FAVORITES FOR ACCORDION
arr. Gary Meisner

20 Latin favorites, including: Bésame Mucho (Kiss Me Much) • The Girl from Ipanema • How Insensitive (Insensatez) • Perfidia • Spanish Eyes • So Nice (Summer Samba) • and more.
00310932...$14.99

THE FRANK MAROCCO ACCORDION SONGBOOK

This songbook includes arrangements and recordings of 15 standards and original songs from legendary jazz accordionist Frank Marocco, including: All the Things You Are • Autumn Leaves • Beyond the Sea • Moon River • Moonlight in Vermont • Stormy Weather (Keeps Rainin' All the Time) • and more!
00233441 Book/Online Audio...............$19.99

POP STANDARDS FOR ACCORDION
Arrangements of 20 Classic Songs

20 classic pop standards arranged for accordion are included in this collection: Annie's Song • Chances Are • For Once in My Life • Help Me Make It Through the Night • My Cherie Amour • Ramblin' Rose • (Sittin' On) The Dock of the Bay • That's Amore (That's Love) • Unchained Melody • and more.
00254822 ....$14.99

POLKA FAVORITES
arr. Kenny Kotwitz

An exciting new collection of 16 songs, including: Beer Barrel Polka • Liechtensteiner Polka • My Melody of Love • Paloma Blanca • Pennsylvania Polka • Too Fat Polka • and more.
00311573...$12.99

STAR WARS FOR ACCORDION

A dozen songs from the Star Wars franchise: The Imperial March (Darth Vader's Theme) • Luke and Leia • March of the Resistance • Princess Leia's Theme • Rey's Theme • Star Wars (Main Theme) • and more.
00157380 ....$14.99

TANGOS FOR ACCORDION
arr. Gary Meisner

Every accordionist needs to know some tangos! Here are 15 favorites: Amapola (Pretty Little Poppy) • Aquellos Ojos Verdes (Green Eyes) • Hernando's Hideaway • Jalousie (Jealousy) • Kiss of Fire • La Cumparsita (The Masked One) • Quizás, Quizás, Quizás (Perhaps, Perhaps, Perhaps) • The Rain in Spain • Tango of Roses • Whatever Lola Wants (Lola Gets) • and more!
00122252 ....$9.99

3-CHORD SONGS FOR ACCORDION
arr. Gary Meisner

Here are nearly 30 songs that are easy to play but still sound great! Includes: Amazing Grace • Can Can • Danny Boy • For He's a Jolly Good Fellow • He's Got the Whole World in His Hands • Just a Closer Walk with Thee • La Paloma Blanca (The White Dove) • My Country, 'Tis of Thee • Ode to Joy • Oh! Susanna • Yankee Doodle • The Yellow Rose of Texas • and more.
00312104 ....$12.99

LAWRENCE WELK'S POLKA FOLIO

More than 50 famous polkas, schottisches and waltzes arranged for piano and accordion, including: Blue Eyes • Budweiser Polka • Clarinet Polka • Cuckoo Polka • The Dove Polka • Draw One Polka • Gypsy Polka • Helena Polka • International Waltzes • Let's Have Another One • Schnitzelbank • Shuffle Schottische • Squeeze Box Polka • Waldteuful Waltzes • and more.
00123218...$12.99

HAL•LEONARD®
Visit Hal Leonard Online at
www.halleonard.com

THE ULTIMATE COLLECTION OF
FAKE BOOKS

The Real Book – Sixth Edition

Hal Leonard proudly presents the first legitimate and legal editions of these books ever produced. These bestselling titles are mandatory for anyone who plays jazz! Over 400 songs, including: All By Myself • Dream a Little Dream of Me • God Bless the Child • Like Someone in Love • When I Fall in Love • and more.

00240221 Volume 1, C Instruments.................$45.00
00240224 Volume 1, B♭ Instruments..............$45.00
00240225 Volume 1, E♭ Instruments..............$45.00
00240226 Volume 1, BC Instruments..............$45.00

**Go to halleonard.com
to view all *Real Books* available**

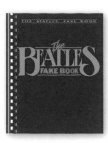

The Beatles Fake Book

200 of the Beatles' hits: All You Need Is Love • Blackbird • Can't Buy Me Love • Day Tripper • Eleanor Rigby • The Fool on the Hill • Hey Jude • In My Life • Let It Be • Michelle • Norwegian Wood (This Bird Has Flown) • Penny Lane • Revolution • She Loves You • Twist and Shout • With a Little Help from My Friends • Yesterday • and many more!
00240069 C Instruments...........$39.99

The Best Fake Book Ever

More than 1,000 songs from all styles of music: All My Loving • At the Hop • Cabaret • Dust in the Wind • Fever • Hello, Dolly • Hey Jude • King of the Road • Longer • Misty • Route 66 • Sentimental Journey • Somebody • Song Sung Blue • Spinning Wheel • Unchained Melody • We Will Rock You • What a Wonderful World • Wooly Bully • Y.M.C.A. • and more.
00290239 C Instruments........................$49.99
00240084 E♭ Instruments......................$49.95

The Celtic Fake Book

Over 400 songs from Ireland, Scotland and Wales: Auld Lang Syne • Barbara Allen • Danny Boy • Finnegan's Wake • The Galway Piper • Irish Rover • Loch Lomond • Molly Malone • My Bonnie Lies Over the Ocean • My Wild Irish Rose • That's an Irish Lullaby • and more. Includes Gaelic lyrics where applicable and a pronunciation guide.
00240153 C Instruments...........$25.00

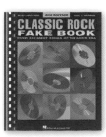

Classic Rock Fake Book

Over 250 of the best rock songs of all time: American Woman • Beast of Burden • Carry On Wayward Son • Dream On • Free Ride • Hurts So Good • I Shot the Sheriff • Layla • My Generation • Nights in White Satin • Owner of a Lonely Heart • Rhiannon • Roxanne • Summer of '69 • We Will Rock You • You Ain't Seen Nothin' Yet • and lots more!
00240108 C Instruments.........................$35.00

Classical Fake Book

This unprecedented, amazingly comprehensive reference includes over 850 classical themes and melodies for all classical music lovers. Includes everything from Renaissance music to Vivaldi and Mozart to Mendelssohn. Lyrics in the original language are included when appropriate.
00240044................$39.99

The Disney Fake Book

Even more Disney favorites, including: The Bare Necessities • Can You Feel the Love Tonight • Circle of Life • How Do You Know? • Let It Go • Part of Your World • Reflection • Some Day My Prince Will Come • When I See an Elephant Fly • You'll Be in My Heart • and many more.
00175311 C Instruments...........$34.99
Disney characters & artwork TM & © 2021 Disney

The Folksong Fake Book

Over 1,000 folksongs: Bury Me Not on the Lone Prairie • Clementine • The Erie Canal • Go, Tell It on the Mountain • Home on the Range • Kumbaya • Michael Row the Boat Ashore • Shenandoah • Simple Gifts • Swing Low, Sweet Chariot • When Johnny Comes Marching Home • Yankee Doodle • and many more.
00240151 ....$34.99

The Hal Leonard Real Jazz Standards Fake Book

Over 250 standards in easy-to-read authentic hand-written jazz engravings: Ain't Misbehavin' • Blue Skies • Crazy He Calls Me • Desafinado (Off Key) • Fever • How High the Moon • It Don't Mean a Thing (If It Ain't Got That Swing) • Lazy River • Mood Indigo • Old Devil Moon • Route 66 • Satin Doll • Witchcraft • and more.
00240161 C Instruments......................$45.00

The Hymn Fake Book

Nearly 1,000 multi-denominational hymns perfect for church musicians or hobbyists: Amazing Grace • Christ the Lord Is Risen Today • For the Beauty of the Earth • It Is Well with My Soul • A Mighty Fortress Is Our God • O for a Thousand Tongues to Sing • Praise to the Lord, the Almighty • Take My Life and Let It Be • What a Friend We Have in Jesus • and hundreds more!
00240145 C Instruments......................$29.99

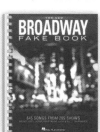

The New Broadway Fake Book

This amazing collection includes 645 songs from 285 shows: All I Ask of You • Any Dream Will Do • Close Every Door • Consider Yourself • Dancing Queen • Mack the Knife • Mamma Mia • Memory • The Phantom of the Opera • Popular • Strike up the Band • and more!
00138905 C Instruments............$45.00

The Praise & Worship Fake Book

Over 400 songs including: Amazing Grace (My Chains Are Gone) • Cornerstone • Everlasting God • Great Are You Lord • In Christ Alone • Mighty to Save • Open the Eyes of My Heart • Shine, Jesus, Shine • This Is Amazing Grace • and more.
00160838 C Instruments...........$39.99
00240324 B♭ Instruments.........$34.99

Three Chord Songs Fake Book

200 classic and contemporary 3-chord tunes in melody/lyric/chord format: Ain't No Sunshine • Bang a Gong (Get It On) • Cold, Cold Heart • Don't Worry, Be Happy • Give Me One Reason • I Got You (I Feel Good) • Kiss • Me and Bobby McGee • Rock This Town • Werewolves of London • You Don't Mess Around with Jim • and more.
00240387................$34.99

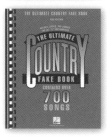

The Ultimate Christmas Fake Book

The 6th edition of this bestseller features over 270 traditional and contemporary Christmas hits: Have Yourself a Merry Little Christmas • I'll Be Home for Christmas O Come, All Ye Faithful (Adeste Fideles) • Santa Baby • Winter Wonderland • and more.
00147215 C Instruments...........$30.00

The Ultimate Country Fake Book

This book includes over 700 of your favorite country hits: Always on My Mind • Boot Scootin' Boogie • Crazy • Down at the Twist and Shout • Forever and Ever, Amen • Friends in Low Places • The Gambler • Jambalaya • King of the Road • Sixteen Tons • There's a Tear in My Beer • Your Cheatin' Heart • and hundreds more.
00240049 C Instruments......................$49.99

The Ultimate Fake Book

Includes over 1,200 hits: Blue Skies • Body and Soul • Endless Love • Isn't It Romantic? • Memory • Mona Lisa • Moon River • Operator • Piano Man • Roxanne • Satin Doll • Shout • Small World • Smile • Speak Softly, Love • Strawberry Fields Forever • Tears in Heaven • Unforgettable • hundreds more!
00240024 C Instruments...........$55.00
00240026 B♭ Instruments.................$49.95

The Ultimate Jazz Fake Book

This must-own collection includes 635 songs spanning all jazz styles from more than 9 decades. Songs include: Maple Leaf Rag • Basin Street Blues • A Night in Tunisia • Lullaby of Birdland • The Girl from Ipanema • Bag's Groove • I Can't Get Started • All the Things You Are • and many more!
00240079 C Instruments...............$45.00
00240080 B♭ Instruments...................$45.00
00240081 E♭ Instruments...................$45.00

The Ultimate Rock Pop Fake Book

This amazing collection features nearly 550 rock and pop hits: American Pie • Bohemian Rhapsody • Born to Be Wild • Clocks • Dancing with Myself • Eye of the Tiger • Proud Mary • Rocket Man • Should I Stay or Should I Go • Total Eclipse of the Heart • Unchained Melody • When Doves Cry • Y.M.C.A. • You Raise Me Up • and more.
00240310 C Instruments.........................$39.99

**Complete songlists available online at
www.halleonard.com**

HAL•LEONARD®